TABLE OF CONTENTS

➤◆❖◆◀

Unless otherwise indicated, all Scripture quotations are taken from the King James Version of the Bible.

7 Laws I Wish Every Protégé Knew · ISBN 1-56394-534-7/B-347

Copyright © 2010 by **MIKE MURDOCK**

Publisher/Editor: Deborah Murdock Johnson

Published by The Wisdom Center · 4051 Denton Hwy. · Ft. Worth, Texas 76117

1-817-759-BOOK · 1-817-759-2665 · 1-817-759-0300

MikeMurdockBooks.com

Mentorship Is...

Wisdom Without The *Pain.*

-*MIKE MURDOCK*

Why I Wrote This Book

Wisdom Is...The Master Key To Life.

Wisdom is the Scriptural solution to any problem you are facing. "Wisdom is the principal thing; therefore get Wisdom: and with all thy getting get understanding. Exalt her, and she shall promote thee: she shall bring thee to honor when thou dost embrace her. She shall give to thine head an ornament of grace: a crown of glory shall she deliver to thee," (Proverbs 4:7-9).

Wisdom Is...The Ability To Recognize Difference.

Honor Is...The Willingness To Reward Someone For Their Difference.

A *man's* greatest craving is *significance.*

A *woman's* greatest need is *security.*

Wisdom meets both the need of the woman... *security,* and the need of the man...*significance.* "When thou goest, thy steps shall not be straitened; and when thou runnest, thou shalt not stumble," (Proverbs 4:12).

The essence of life is instructions. "Take fast hold of instruction; let her not go: keep her; for she is thy life," (Proverbs 4:13).

God is a God of instructions.

The first thing God gave Adam and Eve in The Garden was instruction. "And the Lord God commanded the man, saying, Of every tree of the garden thou mayest freely eat: But of the tree of the knowledge of good and evil, thou shalt not eat of it: for in the day that thou eatest thereof thou shalt surely die," (Genesis 2:16).

Instructions are clues to joy.

An instruction proves caring.

An instruction can be a veiled or subtle *warning*. If you *resent* instructions, life will become very *difficult* for you. If you *doubt* instruction, you will schedule *tragedies*.

Traffic lights.

Stop signs.

Yield signs.

Slow down signs.

Curve ahead signs.

Road signs are *instructions*.

A Protégé Is A Learner.

A Protégé is not a copycat.

A Protégé is a passionate *seeker* of knowledge.

Mentorship Is...The Impartation of Knowledge.

Mentorship Is...Knowledge Gained Through The Experience And Pain of Another.

Mentorship Is...Wisdom Without The Pain.

Mentorship Is...The Shortest Way To Success.

Mentorship Creates Success Without The Waiting Time.

Mentorship Is...Learning Through The Pain of Another.

Mentorship Is...Learning Through The Losses Another Person Has Experienced.

Mentorship Is...Success Without The Pain of Experimentation.

What matters to you most decides who listens to you. People *listen* to you relative to their *need*.

I was chewing a protein bar the other night. Suddenly, it felt as if there was a little rock in the bar.

I thought, "I need to call the company and tell them they left a little rock in this protein bar."

After a while, I realized it was not a rock. I had *broken* a tooth. Suddenly, I was *in love* with dentists. *Thank God for dentists.* I had not thought of dentists in months. All of a sudden, I was now looking for one. I adapted because of my pain and need. My Mentorship focus changed.

Mentorship is chosen *relative* to your goals.

That is why I wrote this book.

Mike Murdock

The *Pursuit* of The Mentor
Reveals
The *Passion* of The Protégé.

-MIKE MURDOCK

What I Wish Every Protégé Knew

————————▷•◦•◁————————

People Will Listen When They Hurt.
There are people who will never listen to you until they hit a very difficult place. *The Reward of Pain Is The Willingness To Listen.*

One day, Dr. Oral Roberts said to me, "The only time people ever write me is when nothing else has worked in their life. When people write me a letter, they have tried everything on earth. I am the last person they come to, and they need a Miracle."

Develop the ability to understand the needs of people around you.

Demas Shakarian was a long-time friend of mine. He was a multimillionaire who had a phenomenal experience with The Holy Spirit and then went on to start the worldwide organization, The Full Gospel Businessmen's Fellowship. His son, Richard, and I were talking in California about how his father always emphasized, "Never talk to someone until they were ready to listen." You waste your energy and time, and create a painful experience for yourself.

Wait until someone is *ready* to listen.
Humility Births A Willingness To Listen.

Colonel Sanders And The Young Businessman

Gary McDuff, a long-time friend of mine, used to

travel with me. He played drums for Elvis Presley. He is a phenomenal creative inventor.

At 17 years old, he *already* had his own business. In no time, he had $17 million in the bank and was living off the interest every month.

He was only 20 years old at the time.

Colonel Sanders, the multimillionaire, was saved under the ministry of one of his uncles in Louisville, Kentucky. His uncle called Colonel Sanders and said, "My nephew, Gary, is starting a business. He would like to spend a couple of days with you." The Colonel agreed.

At about 6 o'clock that night he started talking. He talked and talked about everything he wanted to do and achieve. At 9 o'clock, the Colonel got up from his rocking chair, looked at his clock and started walking up the stairs. He said, "Son, it is 9 o'clock. I will see you tomorrow. When you get ready to listen, let me know."

Imagine being in the presence of Colonel Sanders, worth hundreds of millions of dollars, who had done something no one else had ever done, and all you want to do is talk.

Your Goals Choose Who You Listen To.

What Excited You Yesterday May Not Excite You Tomorrow

I feel like the Lord is making changes in my ministry. You know He is making changes when what *excited* you Yesterday does not excite you any more. You know there is a change when the *thrill* of Yesterday has dwindled to *nothing,* and yet you know you have an Assignment on the earth.

As a young preacher, as I would see stadiums filled with people, I would think, "Oh, I want to reach the world. I want to be like that. I want to do that like Billy Graham does. I want to reach these people."

There came a time in my ministry where crowds meant absolutely *nothing*. I realized that God had *changed* my focus. Chickens eat differently than the eagles.

Eagles And Chickens Have Different Conversations.

God has put something in my heart for the heart of the eagle. The DNA of an eagle is in my spirit. I have decided I will let God handle the chickens and the ducks. There are many who enjoy feeding chickens, but I decided I wanted to deal with eagles.

Your Joy Will Be Complete Wherever God Has Assigned You

As God began to stir my heart, I remembered more than one pastor saying, "You do realize that what you are teaching is over everybody's head."

I replied, "Well, it should not be. I am very clear." I would have this conversation over and over until finally I realized, there is food for *different* people, and you have got to know where God has assigned you for your joy to be *complete*. I have spent enough of my life dealing with masses of people.

There are Protégés like Ruth, who *discerned* something was in Naomi that would *birth* her Future. "And she said, Behold, thy sister in law is gone back unto her people, and unto her gods: return thou after thy sister in law. And Ruth said, Intreat me not to leave thee, or to return from following after thee: for whither thou goest, I will go; and where thou lodgest, I will lodge: thy people shall be my people, and thy God my God: Where thou diest, will I die, and there will I be buried: the Lord do so to me, and more also, if ought but death part thee and me," (Ruth 1:15-17).

Elisha Chose To Stay Close To Elijah

Elisha stayed close to the nurturing environment of Elijah despite the sneering of the other young preachers. I heard one preacher say that Elisha washed the hands of Elijah for *22 years.*

The day came when Elijah said, "Thank you for following me here. I appreciate it, but now some things are changing. You remain here."

He might have said, "I do not have any more food for you. I have nothing to pay you, but God has sent me to a completely different place. It is something you may not adapt to, something you may not like. So you remain here."

Elisha replied, "No, wherever you go, I will go. I want your voice to be the dominant voice in my ear. I am willing to stay close."

Elisha chose to stay close to Elijah. "And Elijah said unto Elisha, Tarry here, I pray thee; for the Lord hath sent me to Beth–el. And Elisha said unto him, As the Lord liveth, and as thy soul liveth, I will not leave thee. So they went down to Beth–el," (2 Kings 2:2).

Parasite or Protégé..?

The parasite is different from the Protégé.
The parasite wants the Mentor to change his

schedule to accommodate him. Elisha *changed* his schedule to stay *close* to Elijah.

The Pursuit of The Mentor Reveals The Passion of The Protégé.

Joshua stayed close to Moses. "And the Lord said unto Moses, Behold, thy days approach that thou must die: call Joshua, and present yourselves in the tabernacle of the congregation, that I may give him a charge. And Moses and Joshua went, and presented themselves in the tabernacle of the congregation," (Deuteronomy 31:14).

The Protégé knows the voice of the Mentor is the key ingredient to *improving* his life.

The Mentor is not a perfect person.

A Mentor *knows* something the Protégé does not know. The Mentor *sees* something the Protégé does not see. The Mentor sees the enemy before the Protégé sees the enemy.

A Protégé has a passion for what is *inside* the Mentor. I want to spend the rest of my life teaching the serious minded about The Laws of God.

There Is A Difference Between An Experience With God And The Expertise of God

The Bible makes it clear that there is a difference between an *experience* with God and the *expertise* of God.

There is a difference between *The Life* of God and *The Law* of God...*The King* and *The Kingdom*.

The Person of Jesus prepares you for eternity in a *moment.* You do not have to be real smart to get to

Heaven. *You only have to be right.*

Remember the thief next to Jesus? "And we indeed justly; for we receive the due reward of our deeds: but this man hath done nothing amiss. And he said unto Jesus, Lord, remember me when Thou comest into Thy kingdom. And Jesus said unto him, Verily I say unto thee, to day shalt thou be with Me in paradise," (Luke 23:41-43).

In one sentence Jesus said, "You will be with Me in Paradise." The thief did not have to go to Sunday school. He did not have to study Greek or Hebrew. He did not have to interpret Scripture. All he had to do was be right.

He said, "I give myself to You. Would You forgive me?"

You Do Not Have To Be Smart To Get Into The Kingdom

If the thief had remained on the earth he would have required the knowledge of God to protect his experience because of the third voices that become influential.

You are where you are Today because of who you have listened to and who you trusted.

Your Future Is Decided By Who You Choose To Believe.

You will not reach your Future until you *honor* a voice.

The Person of Jesus Creates Your Peace; The Principles of Jesus Create Your Prosperity.

Each Law Is A Door To A Different Prize

I wish every Protégé understood the irreplaceable *fruit* and inevitable *reward* of obeying every Law of God. "Now these are the commandments, the statutes, and the judgments, which the Lord your God commanded to teach you, that ye might do them in the land whither ye go to possess it," (Deuteronomy 6:1).

These are the *results* of being taught The Law of God. "That thou mightest fear the Lord thy God, to keep all His statutes and His commandments, which I command thee, thou, and thy son, and thy son's son, all the days of thy life; and that thy days may be prolonged. Hear therefore, O Israel, and observe to do it; that it may be well with thee, and that ye may increase mightily, as the Lord God of thy fathers hath promised thee, in the land that floweth with milk and honey," (Deuteronomy 6:2-3).

His Laws are connected to our *longevity*.

His Laws are connected to our *joy*.

His Laws are birthing even our *increase*.

God kills anything that does not multiply.

A fig tree that will not produce fruit. "And when He saw a fig tree in the way, He came to it, and found nothing thereon, but leaves only, and said unto it, Let no fruit grow on thee henceforward for ever. And presently the fig tree withered away," (Matthew 21:19).

The man with one talent. "Then he which had received the one talent came and said, Lord, I knew thee that thou art an hard man, reaping where thou hast not sown, and gathering where thou hast not strawed...Take therefore the talent from him, and give it unto him which hath ten talents...And cast ye the unprofitable servant into outer darkness: there shall be weeping and gnashing of teeth," (Matthew 25:24, 28, 30).

Sharing The Wealth Is Not Scriptural

Stripping wealth from the rich to give to the poor is not Scriptural. Remember the man with one talent? "Take therefore the talent from him, and give it unto him which hath ten talents. For unto every one that hath shall be given, and he shall have abundance: but from him that hath not shall be taken away even that which he hath," (Matthew 25:28-29).

Every man is responsible for his own *Seed*.

Every man is responsible for his own *income.*

"Hear, O Israel: The Lord our God is one Lord: And thou shalt love the Lord thy God with all thine heart, and with all thy soul, and with all thy might.

"And these words, which I command thee this day, shall be in thine heart: And thou shalt teach them diligently unto thy children, and shalt talk of them when thou sittest in thine house, and when thou walkest by the way, and when thou liest down, and when thou risest up.

"And thou shalt bind them for a sign upon thine hand, and they shall be as frontlets between thine eyes. And thou shalt write them upon the posts of thy house, and on thy gates," (Deuteronomy 6:4-9).

Your Rewards In Life Are Determined By The Kinds of Problems You Are Willing To Solve For Others.

Wisdom Keys To Remember...

- ▶ *Wisdom Is The Ability To Recognize Difference.*
- ▶ *Honor Is The Willingness To Reward*

Someone For Their Difference.

▶ *Mentorship Is...Wisdom Without The Pain.*

▶ *Mentorship Creates Success Without The Waiting Time.*

▶ *Mentorship Is...The Impartation of Knowledge.*

▶ *Mentorship Is...Knowledge Gained Through The Experience And Pain of Another.*

▶ *Mentorship Is...The Shortest Way To Success.*

▶ *Mentorship Is...Learning Through The Pain of Another.*

▶ *Mentorship Is...Learning Through The Losses Another Person Has Experienced.*

▶ *Mentorship Is...Success Without The Pain of Experimentation.*

▶ *The Reward of Pain Is The Willingness To Listen.*

▶ *Humility Births A Willingness To Listen.*

▶ *Your Goals Choose Who You Listen To.*

▶ *Eagles And Chickens Have Different Conversations.*

▶ *The Pursuit of The Mentor Reveals The Passion of The Protégé.*

▶ *Your Future Is Decided By Who You Choose To Believe.*

▶ *The Person of Jesus Creates Your Peace; The Principles of Jesus Create Your Prosperity.*

▶ *Your Rewards In Life Are Determined By The Kinds of Problems You Are Willing To Solve For Others.*

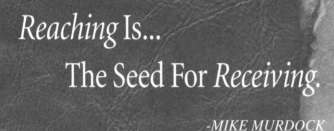

Reaching Is...
The Seed For *Receiving.*

-MIKE MURDOCK

1

The Law of Pursuit

The Proof of Desire Is Pursuit.

A.S.K. Jesus taught it *repetitiously*. "Ask, and it shall be given you; seek, and ye shall find; knock, and it shall be opened unto you," (Matthew 7:7).

Ask for anything? *No.*

Ask according to *Divine* intentions.

Ask according to *the will of God*.

Ask according to Scriptural *protocol*.

Ask the *right* person. Would you go to a restaurant to buy furniture?

Ask *appropriately*. "...ye have not, because ye ask not. Ye ask, and receive not, because ye ask amiss, that ye may consume it upon your lusts," (James 4:2-3).

Jesus said, "Ask of Me." Many times we ask everybody else, but Jesus said, "Talk to Me. Come to Me." "If ye abide in Me, and My words abide in you, ye shall ask what ye will, and it shall be done unto you," (John 15:7).

Many years ago, I was invited to a telethon in New Orleans. There were 24 phones, but nobody was calling. The pastor and his staff kept walking back and forth praying, "Oh God, help us." Several days had passed and *nobody* had called.

What Do You Want The People To Do..?

I said to the leaders, "What do you want the people to do?"

They replied, "Whatever they feel like."

"They are doing it. You told them to do whatever they felt like, so they are doing it. So do not get mad. You told them to do whatever they felt they should do. Would you like for 70 of them to sow a $1,000 Seed into the vision so you can keep the station going?"

"Oh, that would be wonderful."

"Now tell me, why they should do that?"

This was their answer. "Because we are going to go off the air if they do not call."

I said, "Did they ask you to go on the air?"

"Well, no."

"Well, then this is your bill. It is not their bill. You wanted to go on the air. They did not tell you to. You wanted to do it. Now, what did God say would happen to people who covenant with His vision and His work?" I could tell they were preoccupied with their bills.

I continued, "It is very clear. Let us do this Scripturally. Let us ask the people."

"Well, just anything they want." "No. I do not work like that. The prisons are full of folks who did what they felt."

I sat down in a chair and explained to the people who were watching what God said He would do for those who made a financial covenant with Him. I gave them an opportunity to set aside a $1,000 Seed for the spreading of The Gospel so that the TV broadcast could go into homes of people who would never go to church. The phones began to ring and the 70 people called.

The leaders all said, "This is a Miracle."

No, it is called *obedience.*
Ask…Seek…Knock.

Reaching Is The Only Proof of Passion.

Pursuit Is…The Seed For Possessing.
You have no Future you are unwilling to pray for.
You have no Future unless the *price* is worth the *pain*
of pursuit. You must leave Egypt before you qualify for
the Canaan you are pursuing.

It is not enough to *hate* where you are.

You have to know where you would *rather* be.

What is the Future you *dream* about?

What is the *price* of that Future?

What is the *adaptation* it will require?

I wish every Protégé knew the rewards of every
law they obeyed. There is a difference between The Life
of God *in* you and The Laws of God *around* you.

I wish every Protégé understood what they could
have if they were willing to reach for it.

Reaching Is…The Seed For Receiving.

You cannot even be saved unless you reach. "For
whosoever shall call upon the name of the Lord shall
be saved," (Romans 10:13). "Call unto Me, and I will
answer thee, and shew thee great and mighty things,
which thou knowest not," (Jeremiah 33:3). "But without
faith it is impossible to please Him: for he that cometh
to God must believe that He is, and that He is a
Rewarder of them that diligently seek Him," (Hebrews
11:6).

I read many stories of famous authors.

I remember reading about a famous author who
sent over 200 transcripts to publishers, but they
rejected every single one of them. Today, he has sold

over 200 million books. *Pursuit.*

Abraham Lincoln experienced loss and failure in every part of his life. He lost elections. He lost in love. He decided to run for President one more time and he won.

The Future will only honor the persistent.

What Is The Proof of Your Pursuit?

Have you been asking God for a real financial blessing in your life?

If I walk through your house, how many books will I see there on The Laws of Wealth?

Will I see books by Napoleon Hill, Bill Gates, Warren Buffet, W. Clement Stone or Donald Trump?

What proof do you have in your environment of what you are pursuing?

A young man was mad because I did not make him manager of the ministry. I said, "Son, you cannot even manage your department, so why would I give you the ministry?"

He replied, "I would learn."

"Bring me the last 3 books you read on management."

"I have not read any."

"Oh, you want the position, not the knowledge. You want to control people. That is what you want to do. You want to be able to spank everybody. You have got to be a father with several kids to get that position. You do not earn it."

What is the proof that you really want what you tell everybody you want?

Someone may come up to you and say, "Oh, I want you to be happy." Ask them, "Tell me the 10 things I like. You said you want me to be happy, so tell me what you think I like. If you are so obsessed with my joy, do you know what brings my joy?"

What Is The Proof of Your Passion?

What are you *looking* for?
What do you *really* want?
What are you *pursuing?*
Pursuit is how you can read the human heart.
Do you really want a *happy* marriage? What books have you read lately on marriage? Who is your counselor? Or do you just want your wife to obey you?
What is the proof of your passion?
What is the price you are willing to pay?
Do you think a lion says, "I am too sleepy to be chasing that antelope?" He knows he will *starve* if he does not.
What are your children looking for? What you think someone is pursuing may not be what you think they want. The young man that hangs around the gang is not necessarily just looking to be in one.
He simply wants to *belong* somewhere.

Healing Requires Pursuit

The blind man would have never even been healed had not he cried out. "And when he heard that it was Jesus of Nazareth, he began to cry out, and say, Jesus, Thou Son of David, have mercy on me. And many charged him that he should hold his peace: but he cried the more a great deal, Thou Son of David, have mercy on me. And Jesus stood still, and commanded him to be called. And they call the blind man, saying unto him,

Be of good comfort, rise; He calleth thee. And he, casting away his garment, rose, and came to Jesus. And Jesus answered and said unto him, What wilt thou that I should do unto thee? The blind man said unto Him, Lord, that I might receive my sight. And Jesus said unto him, Go thy way; thy faith hath made thee whole. And immediately he received his sight, and followed Jesus in the way," (Mark 10:47-52).

The woman who had hemorrhaged for 12 years was not on Jesus' agenda. Jesus was on *her* agenda. "For she said, If I may touch but His clothes, I shall be whole. And straightway the fountain of her blood was dried up; and she felt in body that she was healed of that plague…And He said unto her, Daughter, thy faith hath made thee whole; go in peace, and be whole of thy plague," (Mark 5:28-29, 34).

Do Not Listen Just To What People Say… Look At What They Are Pursuing

One of my nephews lived with me for a few months. One morning he woke up and said, "Dr. Mike, I feel like The Lord wants me to pursue Wisdom, so I am going to move to another place."

I replied, "Son, you are in the environment for Wisdom right now." I think what he meant was a Bible education from college.

What are you really pursuing?

What are you reaching for?

What is the proof?

The terrorists who attacked New York City did not succeed because they were right. They succeeded because they were *focused*. *Their desire to destroy exceeded our desire to live.* We do not value human life in America. That is why we can get all excited over whales stuck on the beach, but murder children in the womb.

One Sinner With A Goal Has More Impact On The Earth Than 100 Christians Without Goals.

Wisdom Keys To Remember...

▶ *The Proof of Desire Is Pursuit.*

▶ *Reaching Is...The Only Proof of Passion.*

▶ *Pursuit Is...The Seed For Possessing.*

▶ *Reaching Is...The Seed For Receiving.*

▶ *One Sinner With A Goal Has More Impact On The Earth Than 100 Christians Without Goals.*

RECOMMENDED INVESTMENTS:
Dream Seeds (Book/B-11/106 pg)
The Uncommon Achiever (Book/B-133/128 pg)
Unstoppable Passion (Book/B-224/32 pg)

Agreement Is...
The Seed For *Acceptance.*

-*MIKE MURDOCK*

2

The Law of Agreement

One Cannot Multiply.

Two are *necessary* for Agreement. "Verily I say unto you, Whatsoever ye shall bind on earth shall be bound in Heaven: and whatsoever ye shall loose on earth shall be loosed in Heaven. Again I say unto you, That if two of you shall agree on earth as touching any thing that they shall ask, it shall be done for them of My Father which is in Heaven," (Matthew 18:18-19).

According to the book of Ecclesiastes, "Two are better than one," (Ecclesiastes 4:9.)

Two terrorists in Agreement can have more influence than 10,000 Christians who are not in Agreement.

One of the keys to Billy Graham's ministry was sending a couple two years in advance to build relationships with other ministers in the cities or countries he was travelling to.

They built a network on *one* thing. God exists, Jesus is His Son, and receiving Him brings you personal salvation.

They did not discuss The Holy Spirit.

They did not discuss the antichrist or theology. Was Jesus coming *before* the tribulation, *after* the tribulation or in the *middle* of the tribulation?

Instead, they *found* a point of Agreement.

Agreement Is...The Seed For Acceptance.

In every relationship that is sustained, there has to be a *dominant* emphasis on Agreement. "Can two walk together, except they be agreed?" (Amos 3:3).

I have to release people from staff when I realize that continuous exposure to me heightens disagreement. If I am writing a check, I am authorized to give them instructions.

Contention Is A Seed For Confusion.
Confusion Is The Proof A Deceiver Is Present.

Honoring This Law Is Vital For The Success of Any Marriage

Marriage is much more than how much you love each other. Love is seeking the good of the other. Love is seeking the pleasure of another.

There is no hope for a marriage unless you come into Agreement on some basic things.

What is your Scriptural role in the marriage?

The husband is not supposed to sit home and watch television while his wife works to make a living for the family. "But if any provide not for his own, and specially for those of his own house, he hath denied the faith, and is worse than an infidel," (1 Timothy 5:8).

Great wonderful churches have *split* because The Law of Agreement was not honored.

What have we chosen to *agree* on?

What are we *unable* to agree on? Let's put them to the side for now.

Negotiation is built on Agreement.

I Am In Agreement With...The Nation of Israel

The reason Israel cannot give up all their land is because they have a Scriptural legacy, a Scriptural inheritance from Abraham and The God of Abraham, Isaac and Jacob.

There are countries all around Israel that are 10 times its size, yet they want Israel to give up their little piece of ground. Many of those surrounding countries are not in Agreement that that land belongs to Israel, yet Scripturally it does. "And the land which I gave Abraham and Isaac, to thee I will give it, and to thy seed after thee will I give the land," (Genesis 35:12).

The days of America are numbered because there is an animosity and hostility growing in our government toward Israel. "And I will bless them that bless thee, and curse him that curseth thee," (Genesis 12:3).

I bless the *nation* of Israel.

I bless the *people* of Israel.

I bless The God of Abraham, Isaac and Jacob.

I bless Israel because there is already a curse on anyone who does not. I would never bless something God has cursed.

Anybody that does not believe The Word of God is not going to be in Agreement with me. God said those that *prayed* for the peace of Jerusalem would be *blessed*. "Pray for the peace of Jerusalem: they shall prosper that love thee," (Psalm 122:6).

14,000 Leaders Died Because They Ignored The Law of Agreement

Two hundred and fifty leaders, the most skilled warriors of Israel, looked at Moses and said, "We do not like your leadership."

Moses tried to talk to them. Finally, God said, "Move out of the way, Moses. Just step aside. I do not like the way they are talking to you. I chose you."

The earth opened up and *swallowed* the 250 leaders. The next day 14,000 Israelites started a tirade against Moses. God *fried* all 14,000. (See Numbers 16.)

Labor continuously to *stay* in Agreement.

Labor to *honor* The Law of Agreement.

I talked to one of my speakers sometime ago because I heard him say things from my pulpit that I did not agree with. If it is very serious, I deal with it. Not publicly, but later.

I said, "Son, some of the most stupid statements I have ever heard in my life came out of your mouth. Let us go down the list. You thought I was out of town, but I got a copy of your message. These are things you said that are not Scriptural. I am not in Agreement with you. You will not teach this from my pulpit. I cannot allow anything to be spoken from my pulpit that is in disagreement with The Word of The Living God."

Anything Permitted Increases.

My Father's Reaction To Error...

Everybody talks about how gentle and sweet a man my father is. He became that way on his 80th birthday. When I was 8 years old, a young, very well dressed man from Baylor came to speak at his church in Waco. He was a seminary student there.

The young man got up and said, "Some of you believe that The Bible is infallible, that it is The Word of The Living God. I want to show you today that The Bible is not infallible, and there are mistakes in this Bible."

Suddenly I watched my gentle father get up. None of us would want to take my father on right now. He is strong and as fast as greased lightning. He took the young man, shoved him back and said, "We will not have that in this pulpit."

If I even hear of a teacher in one of the Wednesday night classes speak in defiance to The Laws of God we preach in this pulpit, they will not teach the next Wednesday night.

Labor with The Law of Agreement.

Agreement With The Calling of This Ministry Is Necessary For Every Team Member

Before I hire anybody, I require them to watch 3 15 minute DVDs...about 45 minutes...to see if they are in Agreement with the philosophy of this calling and ministry.

I fired a young Protégé that I loved dearly. He had traveled thousands of miles with me. I watched him look at the face of one of the ladies on staff angrily and disrespectfully. "Son, sit down."

He said, "You have not seen the real me yet."

I said, "Well, you may not have seen the real me either. Out. You will follow my cotton pickin' instruction or you can wash cars somewhere down the street for somebody else."

Agreement Is The Seed For Immediate Favor.

Wisdom Keys of Mike Murdock...

▶ *Agreement Is...The Seed For Acceptance.*

▶ *Contention Is A Seed For Confusion.*

▶ *Confusion Is The Proof A Deceiver Is Present.*

▶ *Anything Permitted Increases.*

▶ *Agreement Is...The Seed For Immediate Favor.*

3

The Law Of The Mind

Your Mind Is The Factory For Feelings.
Your Mind *collects* knowledge.
Your Mind makes *distinctions*.
What belongs in your Present?
What belongs in your Future?
If you *succeed*, it will be because you learned how to manage your Mind.
If you *fail*, it will be because you did not learn how to manage your Mind.
Every Failure Can Be Traced To Something That Was Happening Daily...In Your Mind.
God gave you a Mind to resize the experiences of our life. You can take pleasurable experiences and *magnify* them; and you can take offenses and *shrink* them.
Your Life Is Whatever You Permit Your Mind To Magnify.
The Mind is more *fragile* than many realize.
Mental health is *critically* important. The last 8 months have been the most difficult of my life. The fact that I am teaching again is proof that God answers prayer. I cannot even say that He answered my own prayer, but He answered somebody else's prayer.
I had become very *demoralized* that what I had taught was not being implemented. The people I had

spent the *most* time with, in prayer and mentorship, had become like Judases and Doubting Thomases. It was *horrifying* to my spirit. I could hardly bear it.

It was a *contradiction* to everything I believed about the Seed.

You may have sown a lot of your time and energy into your children and then watched them embrace the opinion of a stranger that was contrary to everything you taught.

Your Only Responsibility Is...To Love And Present Truth

If God does not deal with your Mind, you can go crazy over that. God had to teach me that my responsibility was not to change anybody. I do not have a responsibility to understand anybody. My responsibility was to *love* them and *present* truth.

My responsibility is to *obey* The Voice of God, not to change a person. If your goal is to change somebody, you are going to have torment every day of your life. If your goal is to change your child, you will experience indescribable heartbreak.

Obey The Voice of The Spirit.

Let the Seed grow.

Some *sow.*

Others *water.*

God ultimately decides the *increase.* (See 1 Corinthians 3:6).

2 Things Your Mind Needs

1. Your Mind Needs A Focus. Your Mind needs a goal. You need a Dream Room in your house...or at least a Tomorrow Wall.

You need a room in your house where you have pictures of a desired Future.

Your Mind is energized and collects knowledge relative to a dream or goal. The first thing satan will do to destroy you is destroy your hope for your Future.

You may be thinking, "Will I ever get there?"

As you are facing the giants, you may be wondering, "Will I ever taste the grapes?"

As you are getting ready to leave Egypt, and Pharaoh suddenly doubles the hardship, you may be thinking, "Will I ever reach the Future I desire?" *The Goal of An Enemy Is To Stain Your Self-Portrait.*

The God You Serve Cares About Every Part of Your Life

Your mother may not.

Your father may not.

Your brothers and sisters may not.

Your aunts and uncles may not.

Your own children may never think 5 minutes a day about the goals of your life.

You have a group of Intercessors here at The Wisdom Center who care. Two of us are *better* than one. With The Holy Spirit involved, that makes 3. A 3-fold cord is not easily broken. "Two are better than one; because they have a good reward for their labour...a threefold cord is not quickly broken," (Ecclesiastes 4:9, 12).

Your Mind Is A Garden That Requires Constant Attention.

Your Mind Is Your World.

If you do not protect, feed and watch over your Mind, it can destroy you. You cannot afford to focus on dishonor and disrespect. Do not even try to understand the behavior of disrespectful people.

You may be thinking, "Well, maybe if I had said something a little bit different...maybe if I had looked at things a little bit different...maybe if I had acted differently the outcome would have been better."

Do you believe God is perfect?

Yet, when Lucifer took one-third of the angels away from Him, did God say, "Oh, My goodness. If the rest of you angels would just huddle around, let us sing *Kum Ba Yah*. Let us have a hot dog. I am not going to create anything else."

No. *God created us...to choose to serve and worship Him.*

When your children sneer at all your investment in them, do not make disrespect your focus. You have got too many people around you who see the greatness of God in you.

2.   Your Mind Needs A Hero. You need a hero. Someone who has overcome. Someone who achieved what you want to achieve. Someone who has conquered the difficult places you are facing.

I love reading biographies because I like to see what people overcame to achieve success in life.

The Difference In Seasons Is The Giant You Are Willing To Overcome.

Everybody has giants.

Everybody has difficult places.

Your Mind needs someone to emulate. Paul wrote, "Follow me as I follow Christ." (See 1 Corinthians 11:1.)

Knowing the mistakes people have made along the way and what they had to overcome will help keep you motivated.

Andraé Crouch and his twin sister, Sandra, spent a week with me during their vacation. I will never forget the night Sandra shared with me, that at 15 years old, Andraé was so discouraged over a song he had written that he wadded up the paper and threw it in the trash can.

She pulled it out and straightened out the paper. He said, "Oh, it is not worth anything."

She said, "I like these words. This is a good song."

The Blood that Jesus shed for me,
Way back on Calvary.
The Blood that gives me strength
From day to day,
It will never lose its Power.

The Crucifixion has a Resurrection.

There is a *fourth* man in your fire.

God sometimes *allows* great adversity so that others will see we are in alliance with Him, and He with us.

God likes to show off who He is attached to.

Wisdom Keys To Remember...

► *Your Mind Is The Factory For Feelings.*
► *Every Failure Can Be Traced To Something That Was Happening Daily...In Your Mind.*

▶ *Your Life Is Whatever You Permit Your Mind To Magnify.*
▶ *The Goal of An Enemy Is To Stain Your Self-Portrait.*
▶ *Your Mind Is A Garden That Requires Constant Attention.*
▶ *Your Mind Is Your World.*
▶ *The Difference In Seasons Is The Giant You Are Willing To Overcome.*

RECOMMENDED INVESTMENTS:
7 Laws You Must Honor To Have Uncommon Success
(Book/B-294/62 pg)
Dream Seeds (Book/B-11/106 pg)

4

THE LAW OF KINDNESS

Kindness Is A Picture of The Heart.
The Bible says, "The heart of her husband doth safely trust in her...in her tongue is the law of kindness," (Proverbs 31:11, 26).

Kindness is not a *feigned* manner.

Kindness is not *scripted* protocol.

Kindness flows from the *real* heart.

I have many memories of my father. Even my rear end has memories. I could write a journal. My favorite memory of my father is not him buying my brother and me a guitar and a mandolin in New Orleans. It is not my father sitting at the fireplace. It is not the thousands of times he spoke in the pulpit or seeing him with his hands raised as a man of prayer and intercession.

I was 17 or 18 years old. We had a driveway in front of our house. My father had put a water faucet right beside the concrete drive. As I was driving in that night, I had missed the concrete and ran over the water faucet, knocking the top completely off. There was freezing water pouring everywhere. It was about midnight.

I went to my father's bedroom, "Daddy, Daddy. There is water everywhere out here." You can tell the truth, but the sequence reveals a lot.

He did not have the kind of right tool to repair it. He had to find some pliers and reach down into the hole to turn the water off.

You Never Forget Kindness...

I stood next to him as he worked on the faucet, similar to the way a woman stands beside a man who is doing work for them.

I said, "Daddy, I am so sorry."

"Oh, that is okay, Son. You go ahead and go inside. Daddy will take care of this. Get to bed. It is okay."

If only you knew the things he has whipped me over. Smaller stuff. That moment of kindness was worth everything.

I am now 64 years old. It was 46 years or so ago. I am still thinking about it.

You never forget kindness.

Remember Abigail...

Abigail did not sneer at David, "Look at you. I thought you were a worshipper. Look how you are acting because my husband refused to serve you a meal."

Every man I know has a king and a fool in him. The one you talk to is the one that converses back. You talk to the fool in a man and the fool will come out. Talk to the king in a man and the king will come out.

Abigail looked at David and said, "We all know about your greatness. God's hand is on your life. God is going to deal with your enemies like a stone out of a slingshot. You have got greatness. There is no spot on your record."

Ten days later her husband drops dead. David finds out and she eventually became his wife. "And it came to pass about ten days after, that the Lord smote Nabal, that he died. And when David heard that Nabal was dead, he said, Blessed be the Lord, that hath pleaded the cause of my reproach from the hand of Nabal, and hath kept his servant from evil: for the Lord hath returned the wickedness of Nabal upon his own head. And David sent and communed with Abigail, to take her to him to wife," (1 Samuel 25:38-39).

The Magnetism of Your Kindness Will Outlast The Memory of Your Genius.

Kindness Is A Magnet

It is impossible to stay away from kindness.

Kindness is a fragrance like tone can be an odor. You can almost see kindness just like you can see harshness.

Kindness *attracts*.

At 33 years old, my world was coming apart. I remember crying and weeping after my 13 year marriage broke up. I said, "I just need two things. To be a Christian and to be kind."

Kindness is an *aura*.

Kindness is a *fragrance*.

Remember the crowd that wanted to stone the woman caught in adultery? Jesus reacted to the accusations of the crowd by writing on the ground. "When Jesus had lifted up Himself, and saw none but the woman, He said unto her, Woman, where are those thine accusers? hath no man condemned thee? She said, No man, Lord. And Jesus said unto her, Neither do I condemn thee: go, and sin no more," (John 8:10-11).

Kindness is more important than judgment.

Jesus viewed kindness as more important than the *strictness* of the law. Jesus saw something greater than judgment. Jesus focused on what was most important.

A Lesson On Excellence

Years ago I had a little book printed. The emblem on the bottom was a little bit crooked. I was horrified. I invited the printer to supper at the Anatole Hotel in Dallas.

I said, "I brought you to have supper because I want you to look at this. I want you to get out of the printing business. Do not print for anybody any more. Look at this. Look at what you permitted to go to the press. You do not know anything about printing. You do not know anything about accuracy. You do not know anything about excellence. Get out of the printing business. I do not want to reprint it. I have already spent thousands of dollars and look what you did."

I decided I was going to have a bonfire with 10,000 books. This would be a marvelous teaching for my staff on excellence. We would all sit around the bonfire and I would teach on The Law of Excellence...doing things right.

God's work was worthy of it.

As I was preparing for the bonfire, I went to pray. The Lord spoke to me, "I am just as interested in excellence of spirit and attitude as I am in excellence in printing!"

Never Forget This Law..!

There is a time for *discipline*. There is a time for

judgment. Sometimes, we may forget that The Law of Kindness is so critically important.

Say these words, "In the Name of Jesus, The Law of Kindness is in my mouth."

Wisdom Key To Remember

▶ *The Magnetism of Your Kindness Will Outlast The Memory of Your Genius.*

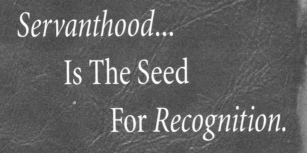

Servanthood...
Is The Seed
For *Recognition.*

-MIKE MURDOCK

❧ **5** ❧

THE LAW OF SERVANTHOOD

━━━━▸❖◂━━━━

True Servants Are Never Denied The Palace.

The wealthiest man in the country, Abraham, sent Eleazar to find the woman who would marry his son, Isaac. "And he said, O Lord God of my master Abraham, I pray Thee, send me good speed this day, and shew kindness unto my master Abraham. Behold, I stand here by the well of water; and the daughters of the men of the city come out to draw water: And let it come to pass, that the damsel to whom I shall say, Let down thy pitcher, I pray thee, that I may drink; and she shall say, Drink, and I will give thy camels drink also: let the same be she that Thou hast appointed for Thy servant Isaac; and thereby shall I know that Thou hast shewed kindness unto my master," (Genesis 24:12-14).

Your Excellence In Servanthood Will Decide Where You Are Invited To Serve.

Eleazer did not say, "Let the woman who qualifies for Abraham's wealth and Isaac's love, be a beautiful well-educated woman."

Servanthood Increases Comfort With Greatness.

Eleazar had one standard. Does she have a servant's heart? And he said, "God of Abraham and Isaac, let the woman chosen for greatness not only offer to water me, an old traveler she does not know. Let her be willing to walk through the discomfort of bringing vessel after vessel to water my camels."

Theologians say it took her hours and hours to water those camels.

The Quality of Your Servanthood Decides The Timing of Your Promotion.

Who have you decided to host on the earth?

Who Would You Identify As The Right Mate..?

Are you single?

Are you looking for the *right* mate?

Some of the most difficult people to get along with sit on church pews. If I were you, I would say, "Who has the heart of the servant?"

About a year ago, I was in Brazil. God was really making the revelation of the servant's heart real to me. I said to the hosting pastor, "Who is a single lady in your church who has the highest level of servanthood?"

He just blurted out some lady's name.

His son walked into the room a few moments later. The pastor asked him, "Who is the woman here in the church with the highest level of servanthood?"

His son blurted out the *same* name.

He asked 4 or 5 people who came in the room the same questions and every one of them mentioned the same name.

You cannot hide servanthood. Servanthood talks *louder* than every other voice.

Servanthood Is...The Seed For Recognition.

Do You Want The Heart of A Servant..?

Lay your hand over your heart and say, "Lord, I

want the heart of a servant. I want the heart of a servant."

I told a young man some time ago who was getting ready for marriage, "Son, do you really want to serve her?"

He said, "Oh, she does so much for me."

I said, "I did not ask you that. I said do you want to serve her? The role of the husband is to serve the wife as well as the wife is to serve her husband."

Those Who Possess A Servant's Mouth Do Not Necessarily Possess A Servant's Heart.

Wisdom Keys To Remember...

▶ *True Servants Are Never Denied The Palace.*
▶ *Your Excellence In Servanthood Will Decide Where You Are Invited To Serve.*
▶ *Servanthood Increases Comfort With Greatness.*
▶ *The Quality of Your Servanthood Decides The Timing of Your Promotion.*
▶ *Servanthood Is...The Seed For Recognition.*
▶ *Those Who Possess A Servant's Mouth Do Not Necessarily Possess A Servant's Heart.*

RECOMMENDED INVESTMENT:
The Wisdom Commentary, Volume 2 (Book/B-220/312 pg)

Divine Provision Is...
   Only Guaranteed
At The Place
   of Your Assignment.

-*MIKE MURDOCK*

❦ 6 ❦

THE LAW OF PLACE

God Made Places Before He Made People.

You must be where God *wants* you to be to be recognized. Even Jesus did not do well in certain places. That is *why* He left Nazareth and went to Capernaum. "And they were offended in Him. But Jesus said unto them, A prophet is not without honour, save in his own country, and in his own house. And He did not many mighty works there because of their unbelief," (Matthew 13:57-58).

Jonah said, "I do not want to be where God has sent me. I am going to go to Tarshish." Out of that act of rebellion came painful days and nights. "Now the Lord had prepared a great fish to swallow up Jonah. And Jonah was in the belly of the fish three days and three nights," (Jonah 1:17).

God's blessing is not just on a *person*.

God blesses you in *The Place*.

Divine Provision Is...Only Guaranteed At The Place of Your Assignment.

I love what Joseph told his brothers. "And Joseph said unto them, Fear not: for am I in the place of God?" (Genesis 50:19).

I am *determined* to be in The Place of God.

I will *fight* a thousand devils to get to The Place God has for me. You cannot afford the sorrow of displacement.

You must be *where* God has assigned you.

I wish every Protégé knew there is a Place of God. If you will pour out your best *where* you are, God will give you the desires of your heart.

Everything You Want...Is Linked To A Place

Years ago, I worked with two young preachers at my house. I loved them dearly. One day I overheard them saying that I was trying to keep them out of their place of ministry and I would not let them go. I called them both in and said, "Who is calling for you?"

"Well, nobody."

"That is how you know. If you do not have anyone calling for you to preach, that is why you are here right now then."

"Well, we could."

So, I released them. They were glad.

I said, "Go wherever God wants you."

One probably backslid.

Several years later, the other said to me, "The worse thing we ever did was leave The Wisdom Center. It blew our life apart. If only I had known The Place of God."

There are people who God has chosen to sit under the mentorship at The Wisdom Center. They may have been offended and decided to go to a different church down the road.

The Only Safe Place Is The Place of God.

Wisdom Keys To Remember...

► *God Made Places Before He Made People.*
► *Divine Provision Is...Only Guaranteed At The Place of Your Assignment.*
► *The Only Safe Place Is The Place of God.*

RECOMMENDED INVESTMENT:
The Law of Recognition (Book/B-114/247 pg)

Honor Is...

The Seed For *Longevity.*

-MIKE MURDOCK

7

THE LAW OF HONOR

Honor Is...The Seed For Access.
What is the proof of Honor?
Politeness is not the proof of Honor.
Silence is not the only proof of Honor.
Honor has a *voice*.
Honor has a *fragrance*.
Honor is *contagious*.
Who have you chosen to Honor?
Your children will Honor who they see you Honor. My mother and father would never talk about any preachers or anybody else. We watched them show such Honor, it affected us as children.

I am determined to become a *master* in The Law of Honor. "Honour all men. Love the brotherhood. Fear God. Honour the king," (1 Peter 2:17).

The other night I looked at a letter that was not supposed to get to me. I was exhausted. We had just hosted a major conference. The letter complained about the food that was offered at the conference. It was not enough that I had spent $40,000 on food. The letter attempted to strip me apart for something that was wrong with the food.

What do you think I felt like doing? She could have bought her own food. She could have driven to a restaurant.

This person would never think they showed me dishonor. Yet, sometimes you and I are like that toward God. "God, I know You did this, this, this but You did not do what I asked for." I want God to help me master *gratitude.*

Make a commitment that *every* word that comes out of your mouth will *bring* Honor. "Righteous lips are the delight of kings; and they love him that speaketh right," (Proverbs 16:13).

There is a lot of God in us. The part of God that needs to be developed is The Law of Honor.

A marriage cannot work if there is no Honor. It is possible to fall in love with someone who does not Honor you. No one can explain love. I do not think you choose who, I think love chooses you. You can be attracted to someone who has never learned The Law of Honor.

I do not want anybody around me that does not understand The Law of Honor.

Lavish Your Environment With Honor

Dr. David Sumrall runs 30,000 in his church in the Philippines. I have preached there several times. He keeps asking, "When are you coming to the Philippines?"

I want to coordinate it with a trip to Hong Kong, because I think every *mission* trip should be accompanied with a *shopping* trip. Hong Kong is just 3 hours to Manila.

The guards at the hotels in the Philippines wear white gloves. They have weapons, but their graciousness is mind blowing. They ask, "Would you be ever so kind as to let me look at your bag for weapons and things like that?"

There are times I have said if I could ever choose a nationality, I would want to be a Filipino, because they were so gracious.

Sometime when you are thinking about people in your life, close your eyes and think of their voice. Ask yourself if you can hear the sound of Honor when they talk to you.

Interest is not Honor.

Need is not Honor.

I do not want comfort without Honor.

I do not want Honor without comfort.

I want a world that reeks with God's Presence.

Watch The Blessing of The Lord Come..!

When you hear the sound of dishonor from your spouse, stop your mate at that point. Do not answer sharply, "Do not talk to me like that."

Instead respond with these words, "Come over here and let us rebuild together. What you just said to me hurts. I really need the sound of Honor in my life. I need the sound of Honor. Would you say that differently?" *Honor Is...The Seed For Longevity.*

Labor for Honor.

Not feigned or sloppy Honor.

Labor for *real* Honor from the *heart*.

You may not have memories of Honor in your life. Learn Honor. Practice it with your children. Teach them Honor. Stay out of environments where dishonor seems to erupt.

Let people teach you how to show Honor.

Honor Must Become Your Seed Before You Reap It As A Harvest.

Let's Pray These Words Together...
"Holy Spirit, I choose to be a carrier of Honor. I will lavish Honor in my environment. I do not want to control everybody in my life. I want to Honor everyone in my life. In The Name of Jesus, I am a receiver today of a mantle of Honor, in Jesus' Name. Amen."

Wisdom Keys To Remember...

► *Honor Is...The Seed For Access.*
► *Honor Is...The Seed For Longevity.*
► *Honor Must Become Your Seed Before You Reap It As A Harvest.*

RECOMMENDED INVESTMENTS:
7 Rituals of Honor That Guarantee The Favor of God
  (Book/B-285/32 pg)
7 Laws You Must Honor To Have Uncommon Success
  (Book/B-294/62 pg)

Wisdom Keys of Mike Murdock In This Book

1. *Agreement Is...The Seed For Acceptance.*
2. *Agreement Is...The Seed For Immediate Favor.*
3. *Anything Permitted Increases.*
4. *Confusion Is The Proof A Deceiver Is Present.*
5. *Contention Is A Seed For Confusion.*
6. *Divine Provision Is...Only Guaranteed At The Place of Your Assignment.*
7. *Eagles And Chickens Have Different Conversations.*
8. *Every Failure Can Be Traced To Something That Was Happening Daily...In Your Mind.*
9. *God Made Places Before He Made People.*
10. *Honor Is...The Seed For Access.*
11. *Honor Is...The Seed For Longevity.*
12. *Honor Is...The Willingness To Reward Someone For Their Difference.*
13. *Honor Must Become Your Seed Before You Reap It As A Harvest.*
14. *Humility Births A Willingness To Listen.*
15. *Mentorship Creates Success Without The Waiting Time.*
16. *Mentorship Is...Success Without The Pain of Experimentation.*
17. *Mentorship Is...Wisdom Without The Pain.*
18. *Mentorship Is...The Impartation of Knowledge.*
19. *Mentorship Is...Knowledge Gained Through The Experience And Pain of Another.*
20. *Mentorship Is...The Shortest Way To Success.*
21. *Mentorship Is...Learning Through The Pain of Another.*
22. *Mentorship Is...Learning Through The Losses Another Person Has Experienced.*
23. *One Sinner With A Goal Has More Impact On The Earth Than 100 Christians Without Goals.*

24. *Pursuit Is The Seed For Possessing.*
25. *Reaching Is...The Only Proof of Passion.*
26. *Reaching Is...The Seed For Receiving.*
27. *Servanthood Increases Comfort With Greatness.*
28. *Servanthood Is...The Seed For Recognition.*
29. *The Difference In Seasons Is The Giant You Are Willing To Overcome.*
30. *The Goal of An Enemy Is To Stain Your Self-Portrait.*
31. *The Magnetism of Your Kindness Will Outlast The Memory of Your Genius.*
32. *The Only Safe Place Is The Place of God.*
33. *The Person of Jesus Creates Your Peace; The Principles of Jesus Create Your Prosperity.*
34. *The Proof of Desire Is Pursuit.*
35. *The Pursuit of The Mentor Reveals The Passion of The Protégé.*
36. *The Quality of Your Servanthood Decides The Timing of Your Promotion.*
37. *The Reward of Pain Is The Willingness To Listen.*
38. *Those Who Possess A Servant's Mouth Do Not Necessarily Possess A Servant's Heart.*
39. *True Servants Are Never Denied The Palace.*
40. *Wisdom Is...The Ability To Recognize Difference.*
41. *Your Excellence In Servanthood Will Decide Where You Are Invited To Serve.*
42. *Your Future Is Decided By Who You Choose To Believe.*
43. *Your Goals Choose Who You Listen To.*
44. *Your Life Is Whatever You Permit Your Mind To Magnify.*
45. *Your Mind Is A Garden That Requires Constant Attention.*
46. *Your Mind Is The Factory For Feelings.*
47. *Your Mind Is Your World.*
48. *Your Rewards In Life Are Determined By The Kinds of Problems You Are Willing To Solve For Others.*

101 THINGS I WISH EVERY PROTÉGÉ KNEW

A Protégé Is An Obedient Learner.

He has a servant's heart. He never makes a major decision without the *counsel* and *feedback* of his Mentor. A Protégé views his Mentor as a dominate *gift* from God...one who has been connected to him by The Holy Spirit for the *multiplying* and *perpetuation* of his Success and life.

The Wisdom of the Mentor is perpetuated through the Protégé.

I believe with all of my heart, *true Success will produce a Successor.* Jesus took 12 Protégés and revolutionized the whole earth. They *trusted* Him. They *believed* in His Wisdom. They *obeyed* Him.

The Uncommon Protégé knows that His Mentor is the *Key* to his Success.

There Are 7 Milestones That The Protégé Will Experience...Potential In Relationship, Planning, Patience, Problem-Solving, Protocol, Passion, Power Transference.

Are you *being* Mentored?

Who is *your* Mentor?

Let These 101 Things Lead You On The Path To Becoming An Uncommon Protégé

1 A Mentor Always Knows More Than The Protégé About A Chosen Focus.

2 A Protégé Never Makes A Major Decision Without The Counsel And Feedback of His Mentor.

3 A Protégé Gets Closer When The Weakness of His

Mentor Emerges.

4 A Protégé Has A Servant's Heart.

5 A Protégé Is An Obedient Learner.

6 A Protégé Must See Himself As A Problem-Solver For His Mentor.

7 A Protégé Puts Obedience Before Comfort.

8 A Protégé Views His Mentor As A Dominate Gift From God.

9 A Real Mentor-Protégé Relationship Will Require Perseverance...Persistence...Pursuit.

10 An Uncommon Mentor Will Require Uncommon Adaptation.

11 Before You Succeed...Your Assignment Must Become Your Obsession.

12 Decisions Decide Your Future.

13 Discomfort Is A Seed For Change.

14 Distrust Destroys Passion.

15 Doubt Is The Thief That Robs God of Every Opportunity To Prove His Giving Nature.

16 Establish An Information System Where You Collect Your Data.

17 Every Mentor-Protégé Relationship Has A Different Plan...Different Levels.

18 Every Protégé Is Still A Mentor.

19 Faith Is The Seed That Attracts Divine Presence.

20 Faith...Schedules All The Miracles of Your Life.

21 God Gives You The Potential For A Future, But God Has Not Decided Your Outcome.

22 God Has Put Something In Your Mentor You Cannot Receive From Anyone Else.

23 Honor Is The Seed For Access.

24 If A Mentor Must Be Guarded In Your Presence, He

Has Not Found You Trustworthy Yet.

25 If You Do Not Take Care of Your Mind, You Cannot Take Care of Anyone Else.

26 If You Have No Heroes, You Will Have No Future.

27 Jesus Never Looked At A Person's Past To Decide Their Potential...He Looked At Their Hunger And Thirst For What He Had To Offer Them.

28 Mentorship Is Learning Through The Pain of Another.

29 Mentorship Is The Quickest Way To Success.

30 Mentorship Is The Transference of Information... It Is Impartation.

31 Mentorship Will Come Through Different People.

32 No True Mentor Will Control or Manipulate You.

33 Once A Protégé To Someone, Always A Protégé.

34 Opportunity Is An Invitation To An Experience.

35 Parasites Want What Is In Your Hand...Protégés Want What Is In Your Heart.

36 Prayer Is Not The Seed For Money...Obedience To A Law of God Brings Increase.

37 Reaction Decides Access.

38 Relationships Decide Success.

39 Servanthood Is The Seed For Transference of Anointing.

40 Similarity Creates Comfort, But Your Difference Creates Your Reward.

41 Something Divine Is Hidden In The Heart of A Mentor.

42 Sometimes God's Highest Gifts Come To Us Through Difficult People.

43 Staying In The Will of God Guarantees Provision.

44 Submission Cannot Begin Until Agreement Ends.

45 Submission Is A Different Seed Than Agreement...It Produces A Different Harvest.

46 Submission Is A Seed That Guarantees The Harvest of Continual Access.

47 Submission To A Mentor Reveals Character.

48 The Anointing You Respect Is The Anointing That Increases In Your Life.

49 The Burden of Mentorship Is Far Heavier On The Mentor Because The Mentor Has To Pay The Price, Has To Risk The Rejection...The Alienation...The Misunderstanding.

50 The Closer You Get To A Mentor, The More Correction Will Come.

51 The Difference Between The Wise And A Fool...Is Easily Discerned By Their Reaction To Correction.

52 The Instruction You Follow Determines The Future You Create.

53 The Mentor Feels The Pain of The Protégé, But He Is Not Captivated By It.

54 The Mentor Knows The Protégé Far Better Than The Protégé Will Ever Know The Mentor.

55 The More Wisdom You Have, The Fewer Miracles You Require.

56 The Plan To Follow A Mentor Will Require Obedience And Adaptation.

57 The Proof of Loyalty Is The Unwillingness To Betray.

58 The Protégé And The Mentor Are Not Equal.

59 The Protégé And The Mentor Are Not Equal In Experience.

60 The Protégé And The Mentor Are Not Equal In Insight or Wisdom or Discerning.

61 The Protégé And The Mentor Are Not Equal In Knowledge or The Mentor Would Not Be There To Impart.

62 The Protégé Changes His Schedule For His Mentor.

63 The Protégé Does Not Decide The Plan...The Mentor Decides The Plan.

64 The Protégé Is A Trusting Learner.

65 The Protégé Is Not The Advisor To The Mentor.

66 The Protégé Will Not Access His Future Without The Mentor.

67 The Pursuit of The Mentor Reveals The Passion of The Protégé.

68 The Quality of The Mentor-Protégé Relationship Depends On The Protégé.

69 The Quality of Your Mentor Is Essential To Uncommon Success.

70 The Reactions of People Are A Conversation About Their Character.

71 The Uncommon Protégé Follows An Instruction Out of Trust, Not Emotional Affirmation.

72 The Uncommon Protégé Knows That His Mentor Is The Key To His Success.

73 The Uncommon Protégé Knows That It Is Only Through Continuous Servanthood That He Qualifies For The Double Portion of Impartation.

74 The Uncommon Protégé Never Forgets That Pursuit Is The Price of Unending Impartation.

75 The Uncommon Protégé Stays Trustworthy In Confidential Matters...In Crisis Seasons.

76 The Uncommon Protégé Will Never Ask For Advice He Does Not Intend To Follow.

77 The Whole Bible Is About Mentorship.

78 The Wisdom of The Mentor Is Perpetuated Through The Protégé.

79 The Word of God Is The Factory For Your Faith.

80 There Will Always Be A Voice In Your Life That You Choose To Honor.

81 Time...Access...Servanthood Qualify You For Impartation.

82 Trust Decides Intimacy.

83 Trust Determines Access...Access Determines Impartation.

84 Whatever You Are, You Reproduce.

85 When You Are At Your Lowest Level, You Can Reach For God's Word.

86 You Are Not Born Qualified, You Become Qualified.

87 You Can Never Rise Above The Mentorship You Embrace.

88 You Can Quickly Recover From Your Mistakes If You Will Be Quick To Admit Them.

89 You Distinguish Yourself Through Attitude... Through Reaction.

90 You Will Have A Variety of Mentors In Your Life...Each With Different Skills To Teach You.

91 Your Decision To Show Honor Will Decide The Seasons You Leave And The Seasons You Enter.

92 Your Future Is Decided By Who You Have Chosen To Believe.

93 Your Future Is In Your Difference.

94 Your Goals Choose Your Mentor.

95 Your Loyalty Is Analyzed By Others.

96 Your Mentor Will Give You Information.

97 Your Mentor Will Give You Motivation, Encouragement And Correction.

98 Your Mentor Will Give You What He Has Experienced To Help You Succeed.

99 Your Mind...Is Your Greatest Investment.

100 Your Present Life Is A Picture of Your Decision-Making.

101 Your Total Addiction To The Voice of The Spirit Is The Only Way To Stay Safe In This World.

"And we beseech you, brethren, to know them which labour among you, and are over you in the Lord, and admonish you; And to esteem them very highly in love for their work's sake. And be at peace among yourselves," (1 Thessalonians 5:12-13).

The Mentor-Protégé relationship is fragile. It requires profound *patience* of a Mentor. It requires incredible *humility* on the part of a Protégé.

The position of being a Protégé, a passionate learner, means that you expose yourself to continuous *correction* because you will continually make mistakes. Never be afraid of making a mistake. Be afraid of no one telling you when you made it. A mistake only lasts if you refuse to *acknowledge* it. A mistake contains *knowledge*. A mistake contains *information*.

If You Succeed With Your Life, It Will Be Traced To A Voice You Chose To Honor.

MENTORSHIP-TALK

1. Your Goals Choose Your Mentors.
   Elisha Journal

2. Mentorship...Should Be The Reward
   For Admiration.

3. Your Presence...Is The Greatest Investment
   In Another.
   Evaluate...For Your Impact.

4. Sometimes, I Teach...To END Your Search.
   Sometimes, I Teach...To BEGIN Your Search.

5. Who Trained You...For Today?
   Who Will Train You...For Tomorrow?
   What Price...Will You Pay?

6. Mentorship...Does Not Create Success. (Judas)
   Obedience To The Mentorship...Decides It.
   (John)

7. The Quality of Questions...Reveals
   The Passion of The Protégé.

8. Your Goals...Explain Your Decisions.
   Your Decisions...Reveal Your Mentors.
   Your Mentorship...Explains Your Wisdom.

9. Your Humility...Decides Your Mentorship.
   Your Mentorship...Decides Your Faith.
   Your Faith...Creates Your Future.

10. Mentorship...Should Be The Reward
    For Admiration.

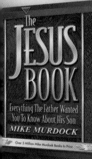

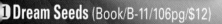

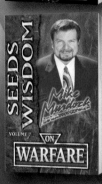

Money 7 BOOK PAK!

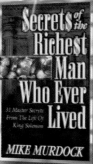

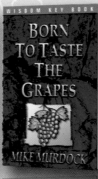

DR. MIKE MURDOCK

❶ Secrets of the Richest Man Who Ever Lived (Book/B-99/179pg/$10)

❷ The Blessing Bible (Book/B-28/252pg/$10)

❸ Born To Taste The Grapes (Book/B-65/32pg/$3)

❹ Creating Tomorrow Through Seed-Faith (Book/B-06/32pg/$5)

❺ Seeds of Wisdom on Prosperity (Book/B-22/32pg/$5)

❻ Seven Obstacles To Abundant Success (Book/B-64/32pg/$5)

❼ Ten Lies Many People Believe About Money (Book/B-04/32pg/$5)

The Wisdom Center
Money 7 Book Pak!
Only **$30** $43 Value
WBL-30
Wisdom Is The Principal Thing

*Each Wisdom Book may be purchased separately if so desired.

Add 20% For S/H

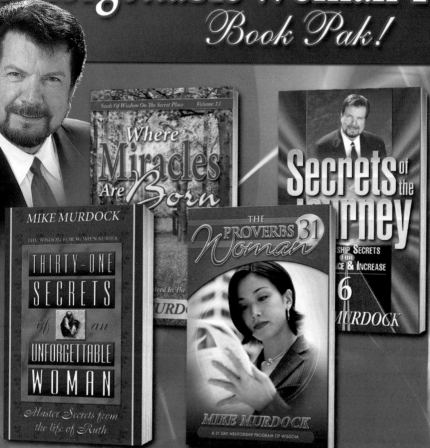

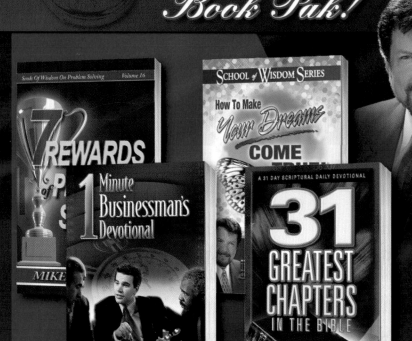

Millionaire-Talk

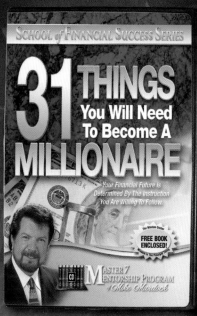

SCHOOL of FINANCIAL SUCCESS SERIES

31 THINGS
You Will Need To Become A
MILLIONAIRE

Your Financial Future Is Determined By The Instruction You Are Willing To Follow.

FREE BOOK ENCLOSED!

MASTER 7 MENTORSHIP PROGRAM
Mike Murdock

DR. MIKE MURDOCK

MY GIFT OF APPRECIATION
GIFT of Appreciation
Wisdom Is The Principal Thing

31 Things You Will Need To Become A Millionaire (2-CD's/SOWL-116)

Topics Include:
> *You Will Need Financial Heroes*
> *Your Willingness To Negotiate Everything*
> *You Must Have The Ability To Transfer Your Enthusiasm, Your Vision To Others*
> *Know Your Competition*
> *Be Willing To Train Your Team Personally As To Your Expectations*
> *Hire Professionals To Do A Professional's Job*

I have asked the Lord for 3,000 special partners who will sow an extra Seed of $58 towards our Television Outreach Ministry. Your Seed is so appreciated! Remember to request your Gift CD's, 2 Disc Volume, *31 Things You Will Need To Become A Millionaire*, when you write this week!

THE WISDOM CENTER
4051 Denton Highway • Fort Worth, TX 76117

1-817-759-BOOK
1-817-759-2665
1-817-759-0300

You Will Love Our Website..!
WISDOMONLINE.COM

G

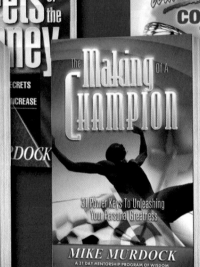

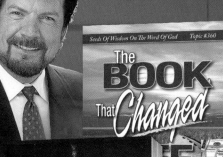

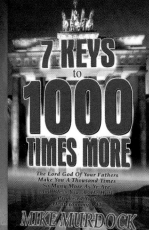

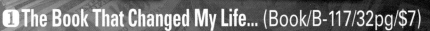

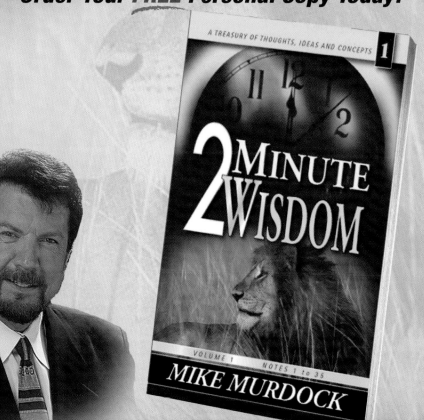

THE WISDOM BIBLE

Partnership Edition

Over 120 Wisdom Study Guides Included Such As:

- ▶ 10 Qualities of Uncommon Achievers
- ▶ 18 Facts You Should Know About The Anointing
- ▶ 21 Facts To Help You Identify Those Assigned To You
- ▶ 31 Facts You Should Know About Your Assignment
- ▶ 8 Keys That Unlock Victory In Every Attack
- ▶ 22 Defense Techniques To Remember During Seasons of Personal Attack
- ▶ 20 Wisdom Keys And Techniques To Remember During An Uncommon Battle
- ▶ 11 Benefits You Can Expect From God
- ▶ 31 Facts You Should Know About Favor
- ▶ The Covenant of 58 Blessings
- ▶ 7 Keys To Receiving Your Miracle
- ▶ 16 Facts You Should Remember About Contentious People
- ▶ 5 Facts Solomon Taught About Contracts
- ▶ 7 Facts You Should Know About Conflict

Your Partnership makes such a difference in The Wisdom Center Outreach Ministries. I wanted to place a Gift in your hand that could last a lifetime for you and your family...**The Wisdom Study Bible.**

40 Years of Personal Notes...this Partnership Edition Bible contains 160 pages of my Personal Study Notes...that could forever change your Bible Study of The Word of God. This **Partnership Edition...**is my personal **Gift of Appreciation** when you sow your Sponsorship Seed of $1,000 for our Television Outreach Ministry. An Uncommon Seed Always Creates An Uncommon Harvest!

Mike

Thank you from my heart for your Seed of Obedience (Luke 6:38).

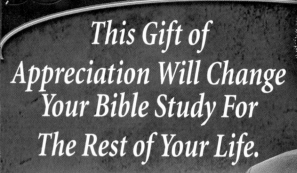

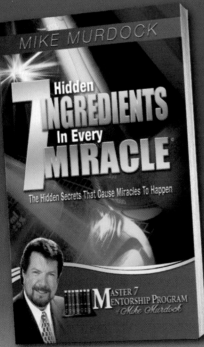

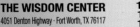

YOUR ASSIGNMENT IS YOUR DISTINCTION FROM OTHERS.

Assignment 4 Book Pak!

Uncommon Wisdom For Discovering Your Life Assignment.

❶ The Dream & The Destiny
Vol 1 (Book/B-74/164 pg/$15)

❷ The Anointing & The Adversity
Vol 2 (Book/B-75/192 pg/$10)

❸ The Trials & The Triumphs
Vol 3 (Book/B-97/160 pg/$10)

❹ The Pain & The Passion
Vol 4 (Book/B-98/144 pg/$10)

Each Wisdom Book may be purchased separately if so desired.

The Wisdom Center
Assignment 4 Book Pak!
Only $30 $45 Value
WBL-14
Wisdom Is The Principal Thing

Add 20% For S/H